ULTIMATE Sleep-Over BOOK

BY K. D. KUCH

ILLUSTRATED BY EVE GUIANAN

Lowell House
Juvenile
Los Angeles

CONTEMPORARY BOOKS
Chicago

Publisher: Jack Artenstein
Vice President, Juvenile Division: Elizabeth Amos
Director of Publishing Services: Rena Copperman
Managing Editor, Juvenile Division: Jessica Oifer
Senior Editor: Amy Downing
Art Director: Lisa Theresa Lenthall
Cover Photo: Ann Bogart
Cover Models (left to right): Samantha Farinacci, Brittany Hendrickson, Taylor Wou Ross

Lowell House books can be purchased at special discounts when ordered in bulk for premiums and special sales. Contact Department JH at the following address:

Lowell House Juvenile
2029 Century Park East, Suite 3290
Los Angeles, CA 90067

Library of Congress Cataloging-in-Publication Number: 95-51383

ISBN:1-56565-710-1
Manufactured in the United States of America

10 9 8 7 6 5 4 3 2 1

CONTENTS

Introduction

SO YOU WANT TO HAVE A SLEEP-OVER?

What's got six heads, twelve arms, twelve legs, and enough energy to light up a city block all night long?

It's you and five friends having the coolest time at your sleep-over!

Slumber parties are great fun. They give you a chance to get together with your best friends, stay up late, play loads of cool games, and stuff your faces with all sorts of yummy snacks. But if you've been to a few sleep-overs, you know sometimes they can turn out to be a big snore! When you think about it, there are only two elements you need to make a really super sleep-over:

- ✔ Fun friends
- ✔ Organization

It's up to you to provide all the great people, but *The Ultimate Sleep-Over Book* will help you with the rest. How are you going to decorate? What games and activities can you plan? And what about videos? And food? This book will help you handle every detail with ease and do away with the panic. After all, a sleep-over should be as much fun for you as for your guests.

So, what are you waiting for? Curl up in your favorite reading spot and get ready to plan your ultimate sleep-over!

Chapter 1
PLANNING WITH PARENTS—A TEAMWORK THING

My mom and dad were really great about letting me have a sleep-over. Their only rule was that we keep the noise down after midnight.

Rebecca H., age 11, Ft. Wayne, Indiana

Your parents may not be the first people you want to help you plan your party. But face it. You need them. And, who knows, they may even have some great ideas! So make Mom and Dad your first stop when you start your sleep-over planning. Even before you begin choosing games to play and videos to watch, you need to discuss the general sleep-over details with them.

Choose a Date

First, you need to clear a date with your parents. Your dad might have a big project from work to complete, or your mom might be planning to paint the living room. During the school year, you'll probably want to have your sleep-over on Friday or Saturday night. In the summertime, when you're out of school, your schedule may be more flexible (although your parents' schedules may not be).

Create a Party Budget

Even the most simple sleep-over costs money. When you've received the thumbs-up to host an all-nighter, write down everything you want to do and have. Next to each item, write down the costs. Don't forget anything. Even renting a video is going to cost a couple of dollars. When you have your budget added up, sit down with your parents. With them, figure out what you can realistically afford to spend. Don't get mad if your parents don't want to spend as much money as you do on your sleep-over. Negotiate instead. Work out a plan to do some extra chores around the house, or pay them back in weekly installments from your allowance. If your parents see you're willing to work something out, they might loosen the purse strings. You can also try a few of these budget-saving ideas:

Limit the number of girls—Eight friends might be too much of a strain on your parents' wallet. Maybe inviting four girls would allow for the activities you most want to do, and still keep within the budget.

Make it yourself—Use your imagination and materials you find around your house to make your own invitations and decorations. You'll find lots of do-it-yourself ideas throughout this book.

Make it a BYO (Bring Your Own)—Ask your friends to bring their own videos, games, and snacks to share with everyone else!

Set House Rules

"Rules are for your own good." How many times have you heard your parents say that? Well, they're right. Setting down the ground rules before your sleep-over will help avoid problems during the party. These are some of the rules you and your parents are going to need to talk about:

- ✔ Which rooms are off-limits?
- ✔ How loud can music/TV/noise be?
- ✔ Who is going to clean up after the party?
- ✔ What time (if at all) must lights go out?

Be honest. You want your parents to help you get ready for your sleep-over. Then, the moment the first guest arrives, you want them to vanish into thin air. If you show your parents you're organized and are willing to follow the rules, you'll probably become the proud owner of "invisible parents." Of course, that's *after* they have the chance to meet all your friends.

> *My mom actually had some cool ideas for my sleep-over. She even showed me games she and her friends used to play.*
>
> Carmen A., age 10, Phoenix, Arizona

Chapter 2
PLANNING BEGINS WITH PALS

I have a sleep-over every couple of months. I invite girls who have invited me to their sleep-overs. And I always invite my best friend.

Crystal M., age 10, Orlando, Florida

Now you're ready for the fine art of party planning. You can't have a sleep-over without friends, so begin by making a list of guests. Deciding who to invite can be the hardest part of your sleep-over. Sometimes it isn't just a matter of inviting your best friends. Money, space, and personalities all should be involved in the process. Here are some pointers to help you make the decision.

How Many Friends to Invite

The number of friends you invite depends upon how much space you have. If you're sleeping in your bedroom, maybe three is the max. But if you're taking over the basement, twelve may be the minimum! In general, inviting five or six buddies is a good number. That's just enough girls to keep the party rolling, but not too many to be overwhelming for you and your family. Never invite more guests than you have room for. Who wants to feel like a sardine?

Eeny, Meeny, Miney, Mo! Who Do I Invite?

It would be great to invite all your friends, but that's not always possible. If your guest list is longer than your parents will allow, use these tips to narrow it down:

- ✔ If a friend has invited you to sleep-overs and parties at her house and you haven't returned her hospitality, now's the time.
- ✔ Invite girls who share a similar interest. Do you have some friends with whom you take dancing lessons, or do you have a group of pals who all love to Rollerblade? There's your guest list.
- ✔ How about inviting a few kids you don't know as well? It's a great way to build new friendships.

Ouch! When Feelings Get Hurt

Sometimes you just can't invite all your friends to a sleep-over. The first thing you should do is ask the girls you've invited not to mention the sleep-over around other people. There's no use rubbing it in, plus it's just common courtesy. But if someone's feelings do get hurt, here are some ideas that might help the situation:

Talk about it—Being left out is hard. Not talking about it might make it easier for you, but it

SMART SLEEP-OVER TIP

If you plan to hand deliver your invitations, don't give them out in front of people you're not inviting.

won't solve the problem. Be truthful. Explain your reasons to your friend and let her know it was a hard decision. Talking is always the best way to deal with a problem.

Give it time—If she's still mad, give her time to get over her hurt feelings. After a while, she'll probably forget all about it.

Know that one party doesn't make or break a friendship—Just because you can't invite or choose not to invite a friend to your sleep-over doesn't mean you don't want to be her friend. She may feel like you just don't like her anymore. Prove her wrong. Plan to do something special with her at another time.

Make It Inviting

For my last sleep-over, I made my invitations look like a bed. I folded a piece of red construction paper for the bed. Then I made a slit in the red paper so I could slide in a white piece of paper for my pillow. When my friends pulled out the pillow, it had all my party information.

Shelly G., age 12, Ogden, Utah

Invitations are an important beginning to your sleep-over, because it's the first thing your friends see. And a special sleep-over deserves a creative invitation. If you're having a theme sleep-over (check out chapter 4 for some cool ideas), match your invitations to your chosen theme. You can make your invitations as simple as plain postcards decorated with stickers, pictures from magazines, or rubber stamp designs.

Send out your invitations about two weeks before your sleep-over. Make sure to include the following information on each invitation:

Date of the event and the time it starts— Include the time it ends in the morning, too, so parents can plan when to pick up their kids.

Where—Enclose a map to your house if your friends haven't been there before.

What to Bring— If you want your guests to bring sleeping bags, games, or swimsuits for a pool party, list these necessary items on the invitation.

RSVP—Include your phone number and a date by which guests need to let you know if they're coming. Give your friends at least a week to respond. Then, if you still haven't heard from them, follow up with a phone call. (Another phrase used on invitations is "Regrets Only." That means you want people to call only if they can't come to your party.)

RSVP PLEASE!

You've probably seen the letters "RSVP" on invitations before, but do you know what they mean? Here's the scoop. RSVP stands for *répondez s'il vous plaît.* That's a French phrase meaning "please reply."

Chapter 3
PREPARING FOR THE BIG DAY

I use lots of balloons at my sleep-over. I rub them against my clothes to make static electricity, and they stick to the wall by themselves.

Andrea T., age 11, Bowling Green, Kentucky

Okay, you've decided the *who, when,* and *where* of your slumber party plans. Now it is time to answer the *what,* as in "What are we going to do all night?"

Prepare a Plan of Attack

Now that you've made up a guest list, it's time to create a list of what your friends will be playing, eating, and watching.

Brainstorm—This is where you put your ideas—any and all—down on paper. You're going to need to consider decorations, prizes, food, games, and activities. (Check out the Party Checklist on page 18 at the end of this chapter.)

Make a detailed list—Based on your brainstorm list, this list should include *everything* you need: the foods you are going to serve, the materials you need for crafts, and the extra supplies you might need for games. Don't forget anything!

Finalize your list—Take a minute to look at your detailed list. Is everything you've written down realistic?

Narrow down your list to what is reasonable and affordable. Parental advice comes in handy here!

Make a shopping list—Now that you know what you need, check to see what foods and materials you already have around the house. Then figure out where you'll have to shop to get the remaining items. Make sure those stores have what you want by calling first. Most of the things should be easy to find at stationery, card, craft, and party shops, as well as large discount stores such as Wal-Mart or Target.

Schedule a parent to drive you around—Set aside an afternoon with a parent to drive you to the stores to complete your shopping. You'll probably need to plan two shopping trips—one for food and one for everything else. (Make sure to also schedule in some time to take your parents out for a thank-you soda.)

> *Once I forgot to buy prizes to give out after the games. Now I do as much as I can ahead of time. I don't want to forget anything important again.*
>
> Brandy G., age 12, Providence, Rhode Island

Setting the Mood

You don't have to decorate for a sleep-over, but it sets the mood and lets your friends know you plan to make this a special night. And to create an extra memorable evening, you can make your own decorations. If you're having a theme sleep-over, decorate around your theme. But even with a "generic" sleep-over, you can come up with all sorts of great settings using the following:

SLEEP-OVER COUNTDOWN

Save yourself unnecessary, last-minute panic by using this countdown.

Three Weeks Ahead: Make invitations.

Two Weeks Ahead: Send or deliver invitations.
Decide on games, activities, and food.
Make your shopping list.

One Week Ahead: Check with any friends who did not RSVP.
Buy or make craft supplies, decorations, and prizes.

Six Days Ahead: Clean room.

Five Days Ahead: Go through CDs and cassettes to choose music.

Four Days Ahead: Make a list for games you plan to play.

Three Days Ahead: Organize prizes to match your game list.

Two Days Ahead: Buy food.

One Day Ahead: Put up decorations in your room only.

Four Hours Ahead: Rent videos.

Two Hours Ahead: Put up decorations in other rooms.
Set up food.

✔ ***Balloons:*** Always a fun idea, and cheap, too! You can tape a few balloons to the door of your room, hang some from string on the ceiling, or write messages on them and let them float around the room.

✔ ***Crepe paper streamers:*** Hang colorful streamers from the ceiling, draped in doorways, or attached to a wall to lead your guests from the front door to your room. Attach the streamers to the ceiling and painted or paneled walls (not papered) with small dabs of rubber cement. It rolls up and rubs off the wall without leaving a mark.

✔ ***Pillows:*** *Fill* your room with pillows. They can be bed pillows, decorative throw pillows, or even chair pads. Use them to sleep on, sit on, or for a midnight pillow fight!

✔ ***Lights:*** Instead of using your regular bedroom light or lamps, plug in night-lights in all your electrical sockets. You may not have enough light to play Monopoly by, but the low lighting is the perfect setting for telling scary stories.

✔ ***Sound:*** A day or two before the party, use a small tape recorder to record friends and family members pretending to snore. The snores should be funny, loud, or weird. When your friends start arriving, play the tape. Let them guess who's snoring. It's a great slumber party opener.

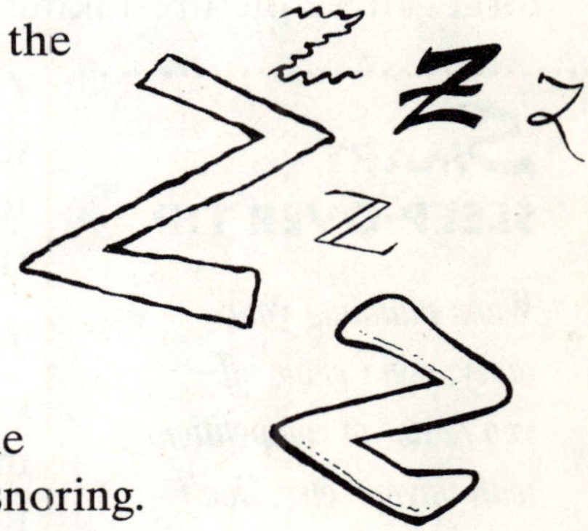

✔ ***Or . . . :*** Is there something special about you? Something that all your friends associate with only you? Maybe it's the colors pink and lavender. Or your love for horses. If that's the case, use it. Fill a room with pink and lavender balloons. Hang horse pictures everywhere. That's a sure way to make this a one-of-a-kind sleep-over.

Make Memories

Save your sleep-over memories. Take pictures. If you don't have your own camera, borrow one from your folks or a friend. Or buy a disposable camera (camera and film all in one package). You can find these inexpensive cameras at most drug, grocery, and discount stores. And don't forget these picture-taking tips:

Smart Sleep-Over Tip

When planning your party, don't show off–you're not in competition with anyone else. Don't overdo or overspend. Be imaginative and personalize your own party. Your aim is to have fun.

Candid camera—Action shots make memory keepers, so try to capture your friends when they are doing something.

Instant pictures—Use a Polaroid camera if you can. They make great party favors to give to friends when they leave.

Make a movie—If you have a video camera or camcorder, capture your sleep-over on videotape.

FIVE FAVORITE SLEEP-OVER FOODS

If you're going to include dinner, here are some ideas on what to serve:

Pizza—Have them delivered or make your own. Mix up your own crust or use frozen bread dough. Add all your favorite toppings.

Nachos—This treat is as simple as opening a bag of chips and a jar of cheese sauce, and then chopping some tomatoes and olives. (Add sliced jalapeño, if you dare.)

Super subs—Start with French bread and layer on cold cuts, cheese, and other fixings. Don't forget to top it with a pimiento-stuffed olive.

Choice chicken nuggets—Pick up a package of frozen chicken nuggets at your local market. Follow the cooking instructions on the package. Then create your own unique dipping sauces. Barbecue sauce with pineapple bits? Mustard and honey? Peanut butter and jelly?

Cheesy potato skins—Scoop out the pulp of some baked potatoes, leaving a thin shell. Cut skins into serving-size pieces. Deep-fry in hot oil until lightly browned (have an adult supervise). Drain on paper towels. Cover with shredded cheese, tomatoes, green onions, bacon bits, and a little sour cream. Yum!

Save your picture—Keep a sleep-over scrapbook or photo album. It doesn't have to be fancy. Even a three-ring binder and plain paper works fine.

PARTY CHECKLIST

Make a photocopy of this checklist or copy it down in a notebook so you don't forget any details for your ultimate sleep-over.

Date of sleep-over: ______________________________

Theme (if using one): ____________________________

Number of girls: _________________________________

Who? ***(Name)*** ***(Phone #)*** ***(RSVP)***

____

____

____

____

____

____

Activities/Games ***Menu***

______________________ ______________________

______________________ ______________________

______________________ ______________________

______________________ ______________________

Craft activity ***Decorations***

______________________ ______________________

______________________ ______________________

Have you bought:

Favors? ______________ ***Prizes?*** ______________

Video rental? __________ ***Camera/film?*** __________

Chapter 4
MAKING YOUR SLEEP-OVER UNIQUE

The best sleep-over I ever had was a Beach Blast theme. We took blankets out in the backyard and built sand castles in my little brother's sandbox. My invitations were written on deflated beach balls.

Donna W., age 11, Knoxville, Tennessee

No two sleep-over parties are ever the same. The food, games, even the decorations and music you use make each one a different experience. When you want to spend more time making your sleep-over party stand out from others, you need a theme. A theme focuses the entire party around one central idea. All the food, games, movies, and decorations are tied to that theme. Theme parties work best when they are based on something you like, such as animals, cheerleading, or anything scary.

All-Night Hibernation

If you and your friends share a love of four-legged creatures, plan a sleep-over theme around animals. Beginning with your invitations, everything should carry through on the animal theme. Use cookie cutters or stencils to trace animal shapes onto colored paper. Write the party details on the shapes. Invite your friends to bring along their favorite animal—whether it's a stuffed animal, a picture, or a book. (*Real* animals must be okayed by

Mom and Dad!) You can create the perfect mood with music that incorporates dolphin and whale sounds, found at any music store or library.

ACTIVITIES

Animal Slippers—Have each girl bring a large pair of white socks. You supply fabric marking pens, buttons, scrap material, and fabric glue. Then each girl can transform her socks into her favorite animal pair.

Worm Squirm—Set up an obstacle course around your house that each person has to get through. What's the hook? Everyone must finish the course completely inside her sleeping bag.

VIDEO

Free Willy (1993, PG, 112 minutes). A wayward twelve-year-old (Jason James Richter) is ordered to remove graffiti from an aquarium wall. There he befriends a homesick orca whale and eventually helps him escape from the aquarium's greedy owner.

MENU

Go vegetarian and whip up your favorite meatless sauce and pasta, served with bread and salad. For dessert, spread a thick layer of green frosting (white frosting with green food coloring) onto a large plate. Then stand up animal crackers in the frosting. Your guests will love "grazing" on this sweet treat!

My best friend had a sleep-over once. Her mom took us all to dinner at a sock hop '50s-style diner called Johnny Rockets. When we got back, we danced to rock 'n' roll songs and watched an Elvis Presley movie. It was a blast!

Janice B., age 12, Sherman Oaks, California

Backward Bedtime

This party may be backward, but you definitely will not be sleeping first! On your invitations, make sure to tell your friends to arrive with their clothes on backward, inside out, or upside down. To decorate, put up deflated balloons, and set up tablecloths *under* the table. Don't forget to have your guests come into the house backward, too.

ACTIVITIES

Backward Scrabble—Scrabble with a twist! Set up the Scrabble board as you would normally and divide into two, three, or four teams, depending on the number of players. Follow the regular Scrabble rules with one change—all words must be spelled backward.

Pin the Donkey on the Tail—Okay, so Pin the Tail on the Donkey may be a baby game, but how about Pin the Donkey on the Tail? Play it just like the famous original, but put up a little tail on the wall and give each participant a large donkey shape you can make from construction paper. It's sure to create lots of laughs! Of course

the grand prize goes to the loser, the person whose donkey's rear end is farthest from the tail. (Don't tell the players that the loser wins; otherwise, everyone will try to lose.)

VIDEO

Back to the Future (1985, PG, 116 minutes). Michael J. Fox plays a teenager thrown back in time to the 1950s. To get back to his own time he must arrange for his mismatched parents to meet—and fall in love!

MENU

Serve dessert first. Recommended goodies include a bowl of whipped cream and chocolate syrup with a small scoop of ice cream on top. Then, when everyone has had her fill, have each girl create her own inside-out sandwich (the meat and cheese on the outside, the bread inside).

The Haunted Overnighter

Why wait for Halloween to scare up some fun? Invitations can be any scary shape you prefer. Use black paper and colored chalk for a spooky effect. Before the party begins, turn down the lights and put a scary sound-effects cassette or CD into the stereo to set the mood. Turn your home sweet home into the nightmare on your street with creepy cobwebs, skeletons, and ghosts throughout the house.

ACTIVITIES

Bodyless Ghost Pillows— Stuff a small pillow form (12 by 12 inches) inside a large white pillowcase. Tie it shut with a ribbon. Decorate your "ghost head" with markers, fabric paints, and jewels. You can make a whole bunch ahead of time to decorate with; then, at the end of the party, give them to the girls as favors. Or each girl can make her own to take home. (Have each person bring her own pillow and white pillowcase. You supply the markers, fabric paints, and jewels.)

Monster Makeovers—When the clock strikes midnight, you and your friends can turn into a host of freaky fiends. Party participants can paint each other's faces, or each person can paint herself. Take "before" and "after" group pictures, and give prizes for the scariest looks.

Horror Stories—No creepy all-nighter would be complete without plenty of terrifying stories. To create the proper scare-the-heck-out-of-you atmosphere, add haunting music and one small light source, such as a flashlight. Plan out a few tales you want to tell ahead of time, then have everyone share her scariest story.

VIDEO

Young Frankenstein (1974, PG, 105 minutes). In this comedy spoof of the Frankenstein legend, Gene Wilder plays the mad scientist who brings the monster to life.

MENU

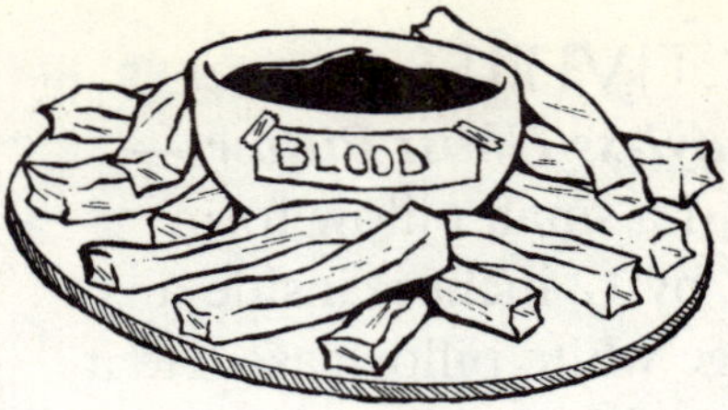

Dish up any meal that goes with ketchup, and serve the ketchup in a large bowl labeled BLOOD. With a little imagination, French fries become bloody fingers, and fried eggs and bacon turn into bloodshot eyeballs and torn-up tendons.

Cheering the Snoozers

If you like cheerleading, this "spirited" sleep-over theme is for you. Before the party, make a large banner and fill it with slogans (Go Team Go, Touchdown, Win-Win-Win, and so on). Pick team colors and ask your guests to wear exercise clothes in those colors. Practice cheering routines. If you have a video camera, have your mom tape you and your friends. Watch yourselves afterward.

ACTIVITIES

Pass the Sneaker—This game is played like Hot Potato. Everyone gets in a circle, and one person stands near the tape or CD player with her back to the group. She will turn on and off the music. When the music plays, pass a sneaker around the circle. Each girl puts on the sneaker as it comes to her, then takes it off and passes it to the next player. Be quick, because when the music stops, the girl wearing the sneaker is out of the game!

Pom-Poms—Have each girl make her own pom-pom with several thin strips of crepe paper bound around a stick with tape. Use them for the cheers you're practicing or at your next school pep rally.

VIDEO

Grease (1978, PG, 110 minutes). Set in the 1950s and full of music, this movie stars Olivia Newton-John as a perky cheerleader who falls for "greaser" John Travolta.

MENU

In keeping with the cheerleader theme, serve stadium food such as hot dogs, peanuts, and soda. Finish off with a giant chocolate chip cookie with your favorite cheer written in frosting!

School's Out—Slumber's In

It's been a hard week of homework and tests, but now school's out for the weekend. Celebrate with a sensational, super-fun sleep-over party. Send report-card invitations with all the vital details.

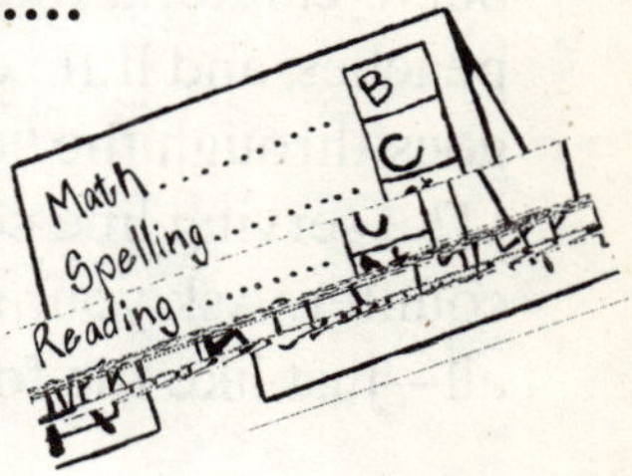

ACTIVITIES

Celeb-ardy!—Jeopardy for the '90s crowd! How well do you and your friends know the latest TV shows, movies, and celebrities around town? Divide into two teams with you as the game show host. Test your friends by putting together a series of twenty to thirty answers. Remember, they must answer in the form of a question! Whichever team gets the most answers right wins.

Yearbook—Buy a plain spiral notebook for each of your friends. Provide them with stickers, pictures from teen magazines, and markers to decorate the outside of their yearbook. Inside, have friends share their best and worst school experiences. Don't forget to have each girl bring photographs of herself to place in each of the yearbooks.

VIDEO

Ferris Bueller's Day Off (1986, PG-13, 103 minutes). Matthew Broderick plays Ferris, who, along with his girlfriend and best pal, takes the day off from school and heads for Chicago in a borrowed Ferrari. They find adventure and fun, all the while trying not to get caught.

MENU

Serve cafeteria food—grilled cheese sandwiches, canned peaches, and little cartons of milk. Make sure everyone goes through the "cafeteria line" with her own tray. (The serving line could be as simple as the kitchen counter. Ask your mom to help serve it—hair net and all—just like the food-service workers at school.)

Siesta Fiesta

This is a fun party to have, especially around Cinco de Mayo (May 5), a national holiday in Mexico. But it's perfect for anytime you want to go south of the border. Songs, games, and storytelling are all part of the fiesta tradition. Fill your room with large flowers made from crepe paper. Throw a colorful spread over your bed. Your local library should have audiocassettes of Mexican folk music.

ACTIVITIES

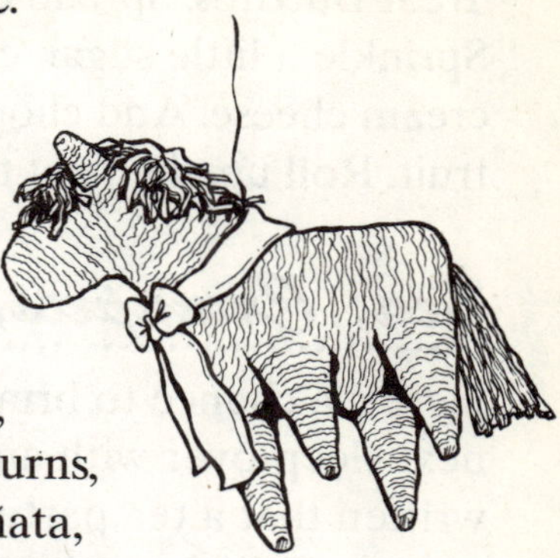

The Piñata Challenge**—**You can buy or make your own piñata, which is a large papier-mâché figure you fill with little presents, such as barrettes, combs, bath beads, and lots of candy. Your guests take turns, blindfolded, to try and break the piñata, swatting at it with a broom handle. Make sure the onlookers are at a safe viewing distance. Once the piñata breaks, everyone dives for the prizes.

Treasure of Guadalupe**—**Put together a list of items for a simple scavenger hunt. The twist is the list needs to be written in Spanish (use an English/Spanish dictionary, if needed). Make up two copies of your list and divide the girls into two teams. Provide English-to-Spanish dictionaries from the library or local bookstore for the translations. (If one of your guests knows Spanish, she can help give clues to the other players.)

VIDEO

La Bamba (1987, PG-13, 108 minutes). Based on the true story of Richie Valens (portrayed by Lou Diamond Phillips), a poor Mexican-American becomes a rock 'n' roll sensation.

MENU

Set up a make-your-own-taco bar with taco shells, meat mixture, lettuce, tomatoes, and cheese. Don't forget to add a bowl of corn chips and salsa. Finish with Sweet Treat Burritos. Spread cream cheese over a flour tortilla. Sprinkle a little sugar, cinnamon, and nutmeg over the cream cheese. Add chopped nuts, raisins, or your favorite fruit. Roll up, then cut the log into bite-size pieces.

Tea, Crumpets, and Pajah-mas

Here's a chance to bring culture and refinement to your next sleep-over with an English tea party (where is it written that a tea party must always be held in the after-noon?). Tell your friends to dress up and be prepared to practice their English accents. Maybe your mom will let you use her china and silver tea service.

ACTIVITIES

Baubles, Bangles, and Beads—Find old costume jewelry at thrift shops and flea markets. Take them apart and use the beads and stones to make new, wild jewelry with glue and some extra pieces of lace and ribbon.

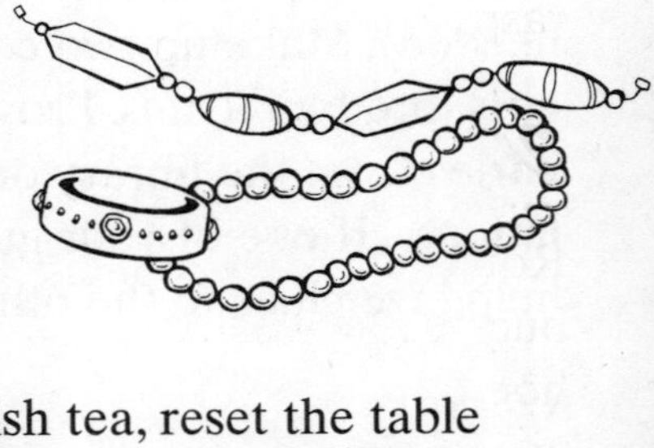

Society Switch—After your English tea, reset the table with lots of things like a vase of flowers, music boxes, necklaces, and other knickknacks. Then divide into two teams. Write down the positions of all the items on a piece of paper. While one team leaves the room, the other switches around various things on the table. The returning team must then guess what's different about the table. Reset the table again, this time having the other team leave the room.

VIDEO

The Secret Garden (1993, G, 101 minutes). An orphan (Kate Maberly) is sent to live with her uncle on a forbidding estate. But she soon befriends her invalid cousin and a local boy. Together the three work to bring to life a walled-up garden on the estate.

MENU

The English love tiny tea sandwiches made with bread and vegetables. Try slices of cucumber on whole wheat or radishes on white bread. Once you've finished your elegant sandwiches and tea, pig out on frosted ladyfingers. Spread white frosting on sticks of sponge cake, then paint on red fingernails (white frosting with red food coloring). Don't forget to serve tea—these days all kinds of teas are available, like raspberry, peach, and mint.

Wild West Rest

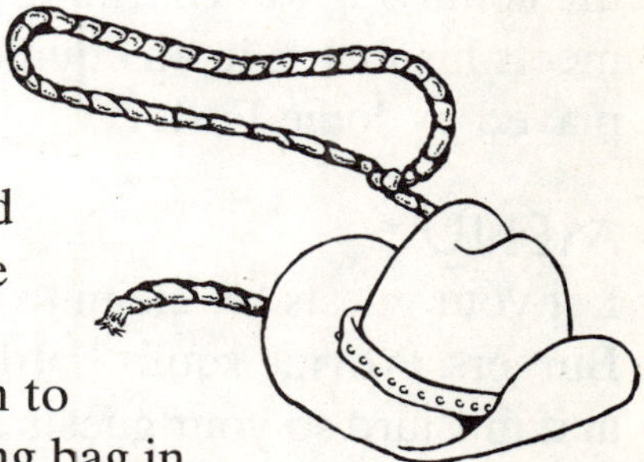

Round up a few of your best buckaroos for an old-fashioned hoedown under the stars. Have everyone wear their jeans and boots. Don't forget to tell them to bring a bedroll (that's a sleeping bag in western lingo). If it's a warm summer night, camp out in the backyard. If the weather is bad, the den and fireplace work just as well. Don't forget to put on some country-and-western music, and rent a line-dancing video to learn the latest steps.

ACTIVITIES

Bedtime Bandannas—Buy a package of plain white handkerchiefs at a thrift store. Then let each girl paint up her own personalized bandanna with puff paints and glitter.

Roundup—Have everyone sit in a circle. They are the "cows." In the center is the "cowpoke," who is blindfolded. Someone turns the cowpoke around a couple of times and hands her a pillow. The cowpoke walks around, and when she's ready to round up a cow, she drops the pillow in front of any one "cow." The cow must then "moo." If the cowpoke can't identify who the cow is, she moves on. If the cowpoke guesses right, she switches places with the cow. Once the new cowpoke is blindfolded, all the girls should switch places.

VIDEO

Maverick (1994, PG, 129 minutes). Mel Gibson stars as the conniving but charming gambler Bret Maverick. He meets his match in an equally conniving young woman, played by Jodie Foster.

MENU

Let your guests lay claim to their own Branded Burgers. Provide squirt bottles of ketchup and mustard so your guests can add their initials (or any other design). Set out a big bowl of trail mix (nuts, raisins, and chocolate chips), and wash down all the chow with lemonade and root beer. Finish up by roasting marshmallows over the barbecue.

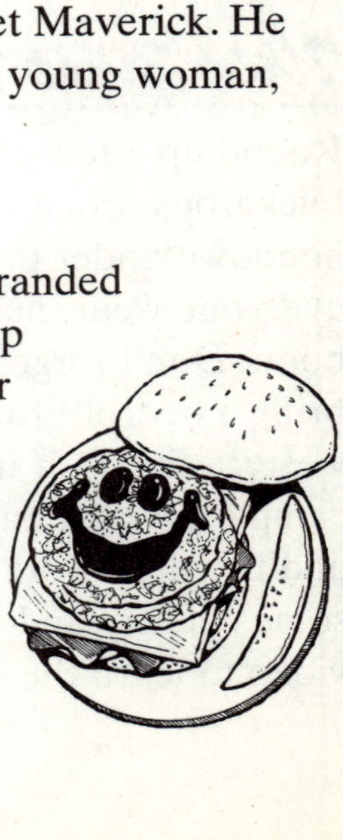

Staying at the Ritz

Make your sleep-over a vacation spot. Post a large sign that says THE SLEEP-OVER RITZ. Have the bellboy (Dad, if you can talk him into it) take the guests' bags to the room where they'll be sleeping. Put a small table near the door. Post more signs directing your guests to the dining room and kitchen.

ACTIVITIES

Picture This—Make your own picture frames so everyone can remember their "holiday" sleep-over. Buy inexpensive cardboard frames at a local craft shop. Provide all kinds of materials to embellish the frames, such as old plane or bus tickets, cut-up pieces of postcards, used stamps, anything that has to do with travel. Either take pictures with an instant camera or send out the developed pictures to each girl after the party, so they have something to put into their frames!

Room Service!—This is a perfect game to play if you can use most of your house. On one end of a long piece of string tie a small gift—anything from a candy bar to a fun pack of little soaps and lotions. Hide the gift in any room under a pillow or behind a bookshelf. Then wind the string throughout your house, going through closets, around tables, under beds, and so on. The other end of the string needs to end up in the main room from which you are starting. On this end, tie a large cardboard key. Create a string maze for each guest. Who can get to their prize the quickest?

VIDEO

Harry and the Hendersons (1987, PG, 111 minutes). The story of a family who goes on vacation and comes back home with Big Foot.

MENU

Take a dip, but not in the pool. Provide foods you dip into a variety of sauces: cocktail franks dipped into barbecue sauce, cut vegetables dipped into ranch dressing or salsa, and pieces of fruit dipped into a sweet cream, such as whipped cream.

LET'S GO OUT

No one says you have to stay in the house all night for your sleep-over. Plan an outing–approved and supervised by parents. The following ideas might take some extra planning (and cost more), but they are sure to make your sleep-over unique:

- Bowling
- Horseback riding (you may need to start the sleep-over early to get this in before dark)
- Ice skating
- Miniature golf
- Movie
- Pizza parlor
- Roller skating
- Shopping at the mall
- Amusement park
- Video arcade

Chapter 5
HOSTESS WITH THE MOSTEST

I take pictures of my friends making silly faces when they first come into my house. It gets everyone into the party mood.

Cheryl F., age 9, Medford, Oregon

There's a lot more to hosting a sleep-over than planning games and activities. You have to deal with your brothers, sisters, and parents. You must keep all your friends entertained. And if a problem arises, *you* have to solve it. It's a lot to juggle, but you can handle it. After all, you're the hostess with the mostest! (At least you will be after reading this chapter.)

Timing Is Everything

No rule says a sleep-over has to be run a certain way. To make the evening as smooth as possible, put together a logical schedule of activities that makes sense for you. But be as flexible as possible. If your friends are bored with a video, don't make them sit through the whole thing. Or if everyone is starving, serve dinner or midnight snacks as soon as you can. Here are some general activities and the approximate best times to do them as you are scheduling your slumber party.

✔ ***Your friends arrive.*** The guests probably won't arrive at exactly the same time, so plan an activity that can be started immediately, and allow for newcomers to join in. Put out a puzzle on the dining room table or set out your CDs and cassettes for your friends to go through.

✔ ***Introductions.*** When someone arrives who doesn't know the others, introduce her right away. Your guests will also appreciate your including any information about the newcomer that will break the ice, such as "Megan's on my soccer team, and she loves old 'I Love Lucy' reruns."

✔ ***Crafts.*** Start your craft activity early in the evening, especially if there is drying time or cooking time involved. Then you can finish your projects after you eat.

✔ ***Food.*** The best time to serve food is anytime! But don't serve loads of appetizers and snacks if you are offering a large dinner soon.

✔ ***Games.*** Games are best when spread throughout the night, not all bunched up in one sitting. One suggestion is to start with a game, then eat. Play another game, then do a craft. Play another game, then watch a video. This is one area where you need to be especially flexible to extend a game if everyone is having tons of fun, or call it quits early.

✔ ***Videos.*** A video is usually best received when it is played later in the evening. Guests are starting to get tired, and those who are exhausted can take a little nap without drawing attention to themselves.

Answers to Those Important Sleep-over Questions

> *When I'm having a sleep-over, my mom takes my six-year-old sister out shopping. By the time they come home, it's almost her bedtime. I let her play one game with us and she's happy.*
>
> Blair T., age 11, Madison, Wisconsin

Problems do arise. That's a fact of life. When something goes wrong, your best defense is to be prepared. Here are some questions that might come up—and the answers that'll make your sleep-over go a lot more smoothly.

Q: *My little sister is a pest. How can I keep her out of my sleep-over?*

A: Generally, younger siblings will cause problems because they look up to you and want to be like you. Don't despair. Before your sleep-over starts, sit down with your little sister. Tell her you want to make it a fun time for your special guests. Make a deal with her that if she won't bother you and your friends that night, you'll help her plan her own sleep-over when Mom and Dad give the okay.

Q: *But what if that doesn't help?*

A: Younger siblings don't want to miss out on the action. If your little sister is persistent, don't fight it. When you pull out a craft, make sure to include your little sister. If you're cooking, give her something to do. Let her watch a video with you and your friends, or even play a game. Make sure she understands she can stay for only an activity or two, and then she has to leave you and your friends alone. You'll find by including younger siblings in just one activity, they'll be happy. It's better than spending your entire evening screaming at her. And remember: To your friends, she's not nearly the pest she may be to you; in fact, some of them might think she's (fasten your seat belt) cute.

Q: *My older brother is always teasing me and my friends. What can I do?*

A: An older brother (and yes, an older sister, too) is probably just looking for a reason to tease you. There's only one way to handle your older siblings. Ignore them. Your friends should do the same. And whatever you do, don't show you're upset. They'll eventually go away.

Q: *It's not my brother and sister I worry about. It's my parents. Last time I had a sleep-over, my mom came in every five minutes and asked if we were having fun. How can I have fun if she's in my face all night?*

A: Sometimes parents get so excited about your parties they include themselves without even thinking. Don't get mad—talk it out. And check out Chapter 1 for more ways to deal with parents.

SMART SLEEP-OVER TIP

Don't push any guest into doing something she really doesn't want to do.

Q: *I was at a party when one of my friends got mad at something, and it ruined the whole night. Is there anything I can do to avoid this?*

A: It is possible for guests to get out of hand sometimes. It can happen when the activities and games get too frantic. Try taking your rambunctious friend aside out of view of the other guests and point out that a problem is brewing. Don't accuse her of being the problem. Give her a chance to see what's going on and come up with a solution together. Don't embarrass her in front of the others—it's not good hostess manners.

Q: *But what if she doesn't stop?*

A: Then call "Rescue M-O-M!" Let an adult be the referee when a situation really gets out of control.

Q: *I have two friends who always try to outdo each other, especially when it comes to games. What can I do to stop an argument before it starts?*

A: It's easy to get caught up in a game. Suddenly everyone just wants to win, win, win. But with winners come losers and hurt feelings. Always keep the mood lighthearted. Laugh a lot and remind your friends it's only a game. After all, you're there to have fun!

Q: *My friend Jan is really shy. She acts like she doesn't want to play, but I know she does. How can I get her involved in our games?*

A: Always plan activities that include everyone. Assign partners when necessary, so that no one is left out in the choosing process.

Q: *I've worked hard to organize the perfect sleep-over, but then one of my friends wants to quit early and go to bed. How can I keep her up?*

A: You may be ready to party all night, but some of your guests may not. Always let a tired girl sleep in peace. A grumpy friend isn't much fun anyway.

Q: *It makes me so mad when things don't go the way I planned. What am I doing wrong?*

A: Be flexible. If a game isn't working, try another one. If the food falls in the dog dish, call for a pizza. Your sleep-over doesn't have to follow a specific plan. The real secret to a successful overnighter is not planning every single detail perfectly, but being flexible enough to roll with whatever surprises the evening holds!

Chapter 6
THE BIG NIGHT

I try to plan games that involve everyone in a group, not just pairs of girls. That way no one gets mad if they're not with their favorite partner.

Tammy R., age 11, Columbia, South Carolina

All right. This is it. The night you've been waiting for. Because you want everything to be perfect, here are several superfun games, crafts, and activities to keep you busy all night long.

A Night of Fun and Games

Everyone loves to play games. Here are seven that are sure to make your sleep-over stand out from others.

READY FOR BED?

Divide into two equal teams (if there is an uneven number, you can be the judge). Each team starts with an overnight bag full of bed clothing: a pair of pajamas, a pair of slippers, a robe, curlers, and mud mask cream. Both bags are put on the opposite side of the room. At the signal, the first person on each team runs to the overnight bag and opens it. The two players quickly put on all the clothes (don't forget one curler and a smudge of mud mask) and run back to the starting position carrying the overnight bag. The two players then take off all the clothes, leaving the curler and mud mask on. They put the clothes back in the overnight bags and return them to their original position across the room. Then the second member of each team goes through the same actions. This continues until every player has had a turn. The first team to finish wins. Before everyone washes off her mud mask and takes out her curler, take a picture of the teams—a perfect photo opportunity!

PILLOW PIT

Here's something to do with pillows other than the standard pillow fight. Pile up all the pillows in a circle about 5 feet wide. Have all the girls stand in a circle around the pillows and join hands. On the count of three, everyone begins to push and pull the other players, keeping hands locked. The idea is to get the other players to touch, step on, or fall into the pillow pile, while trying to keep away from the pillows yourself. When someone touches the pillows, she is out of the game. As the circle gets smaller, you may have to remove a few of the pillows. The last girl to not step onto a pillow is the winner.

FREAKY CREATURE FOOD

Your mom has said it a million times: "Don't play with your food." Well, here's your chance to play all you like. Before the party, put together an ingredients tray. Use as many different foods as you can. Everyone competes to create a freaky creature using unusual food combinations. There's only one rule—after the competition, you

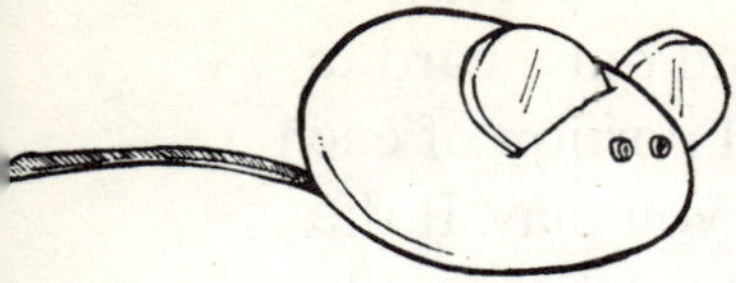

must eat your creation! Try making a freaky mouse with a hard-boiled egg, green onions, and cheese pieces. Or how about a monster face with an apple, peanut butter, and olives? Here's a list of good foods to use:

breads
cherry tomatoes
cold cuts
hard boiled eggs
olives
pickles
pretzels
spray cheese
candies
cheese
green onions
lettuce
peanut butter
popcorn
raisins
tortillas

BINGO BONGO SONGO!

Go through your CDs and cassettes and pick fifteen to twenty songs. Choose songs most people would know. Make playing cards for each player. Use regular typing paper or light cardboard and draw nine boxes (three rows of three boxes on each card). Write titles of the songs inside the boxes.

Vary each card, putting the song titles in different orders. When you're ready to play, hand out a card to each player. Then start playing a small portion of each song. Keep a running list of the songs you play. If the players recognize the song and have it on their card, they should put a small marker or coin on the box. The first player to have three filled boxes in a row (vertically, horizontally, or diagonally) calls out, "Bingo-Bongo-Songo!"

LOONY BALLOONS

Before your friends arrive, on separate slips of paper write at least one silly instruction for each girl to do at your sleep-over, such as "Touch your nose with your tongue" or "Sing a song backward." Then roll up each one and slip it into a balloon. Blow up the balloons and tie them off. When you're ready to play, have everyone sit in a circle. Use one balloon per girl for each round. Pass the balloons around—or keep them bouncing in the air—until you say, "Stop." Everyone takes the balloon closest to her and pops it. Then, one at a time, each girl acts out the instruction. Play again and again, until the balloons are used up.

TONIGHT, STARRING . . .

Before guests arrive, cut out pictures from magazines of your favorite movie and TV stars. Then, as each girl arrives, tape a picture to her back (don't let her see who it is!). Let your friends circulate around and ask each other yes/no questions to try and figure out who is taped to her back. They can ask any question that can be answered yes or no. The first girl to guess her character is the winner. Continue the game until everyone guesses who she is. If it takes too long for everyone to guess, go on with the other activities you've planned. Continue to give your guests a chance to make more guesses every so often. There's no time limit on this activity; your friends can have all night to guess!

TOUCHY-TOUCHY

Before your guests arrive, fill a covered basket or box with all kinds of objects, like a nail, string, a wad of tissues, and an olive. Look around your house to come up with your own ideas. When you're ready to play, ask your friends to slip their hands into the basket. (They can't remove the top and peek!) Let each person feel around in the basket for about a minute. Then give everyone a piece of paper. The person who can guess the most objects wins.

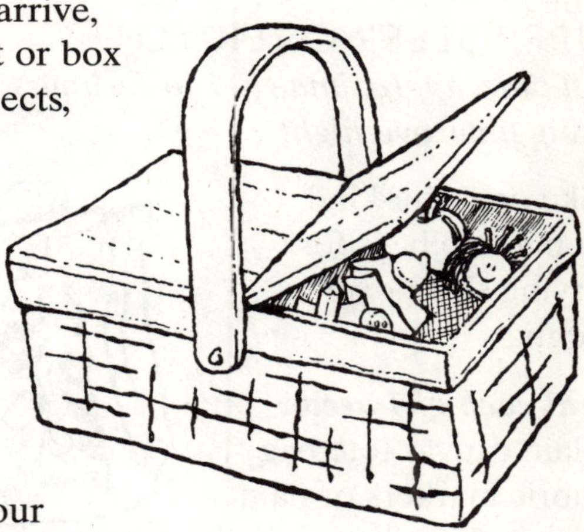

When I have a sleep-over, I tell every girl to bring one game or one game idea. It's fun to have different ideas.

Olivia L., age 9, Newport News, Virginia

Slumbering Souvenirs

If you and your friends love to make things, plan to make a craft your guests can take home as a sleep-over souvenir. The craft store will have all the supplies you need to make the following five crafts. You may want to provide a few of the materials and ask your friends to bring some, too.

SUPER SLEEP-OVER TOTE

craft time: approximately 1 to 1½ hours
drying time: overnight

Make one-of-a-kind pajama tote bags for carrying sleep-over essentials.

What each girl needs:
- plain canvas tote bag
- fabric markers or paints
- piece of cardboard, size of tote bag • pencil
- fabric glue • jewels or beads

1. Use the pencil to trace your own design on the plain tote bag. Let your imagination run wild. Do a self-portrait, draw your favorite animal, or stamp your fingerprints. If you want your friends to autograph it, have them write their signatures in pencil. Then you can go over the writing in markers or paints.

2. Place a piece of cardboard inside the tote bag before you start painting to keep the colors from seeping

through to the back side of the bag. Then paint over the penciled lines with fabric markers or paint. Glue on some jewels or beads. Let the glue and paint dry overnight. By morning the tote bags will be ready to use for the next sleep-over.

STARRY, STARRY NIGHT MOBILE

craft time: approximately 1 to 2 hours
drying time: approximately 1 hour

Who needs a telescope to look at the stars when you can have this starry mobile hanging over your head?

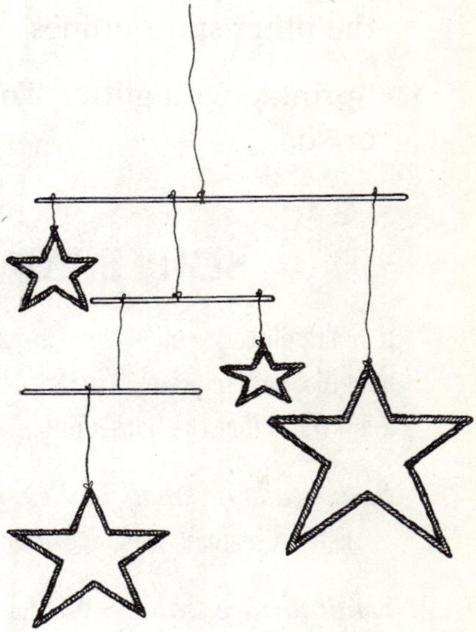

What each girl needs:

- pencil • plain paper
- waxed paper • cotton cord • glitter • scissors
- white glue • paper plate
- two sticks, 10 inches long (wooden bamboo skewers work well, or have an adult cut ⅛-inch-thick dowels to length)
- thin string

1. Draw four star shapes in pencil on the plain paper. Make them different sizes, from 3 to 5 inches. Lay a piece of waxed paper over the shapes. If you need to, tape it down so it doesn't move.

2. Pour some glue on a paper plate, so it's covering the bottom. Cut a 36-inch length of cord. Run it through

the glue, making sure it is completely soaked. Put the glue-soaked string on the waxed paper, following the lines of your star drawing. Snip the cord to close your star shape. Repeat with the other star outlines.

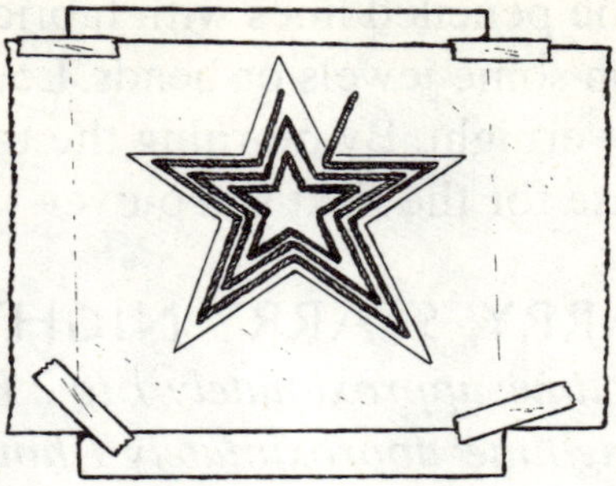

3. Sprinkle with glitter. The stars need to dry an hour or so.

SIMPLE AND CHEAP PRIZES

If you're playing games, there are always going to be winners. And winners like getting prizes. You don't have to spend a lot of money. Here are a few ideas that cost just a little:

Bath beads or small bottles of lotion–Most drugstores have an aisle with small, trial-size bottles of toiletries.

Small picture frames–Wait for a sale and stock up.

Barrettes, headbands, and ponytail holders–Buy packages of ten or more so you have enough to give to your friends and still have a couple for yourself.

$1 gift certificates to fast-food restaurants–Get them from your favorite hangout.

Small plants–Start a friend on a new hobby.

4. When the glue has dried, peel the waxed paper away from the stars and start putting together your mobile. You'll need to cut one of the skewers in half so you have one long piece and two shorter pieces.

5. Tie pieces of string connecting two of the stars to the long piece of wood and one star to each of the smaller sticks. Then use two more lengths of string to tie the small skewers and stars to the larger piece. You might have to spend some time getting the right balance so it doesn't tilt too far to one side. Finish by using a longer string to hang up the mobile.

COLORFUL TOOTHBRUSH CADDY

craft time: approximately 1 hour

Make sure everyone brings a toothbrush so she can use this souvenir right away.

What each girl needs:

- white glue • paper plate
- paintbrush • small, clean, empty can (a soup can is okay, but start collecting these early, or ask your friends to bring their own) • clear tape • various colors of knitting yarn, including black • two buttons • scissors

1. Pour some glue onto the paper plate. Use the paintbrush to smear a 1-inch strip around the lowest area of the can.

2. Tape one end of colored yarn to the bottom of the can. Begin wrapping the yarn around the can, pressing

the yarn into the layer of glue. As you wrap, push the rows of yarn close together. When you have about a 1-inch solid band of yarn, cut it so the yarn ends at the glue. Switch to another color of yarn and continue wrapping. Add more glue to the can if you need it. When you get an inch away from the top of the can, stop and switch back to the first color you used, or try a completely different color of yarn.

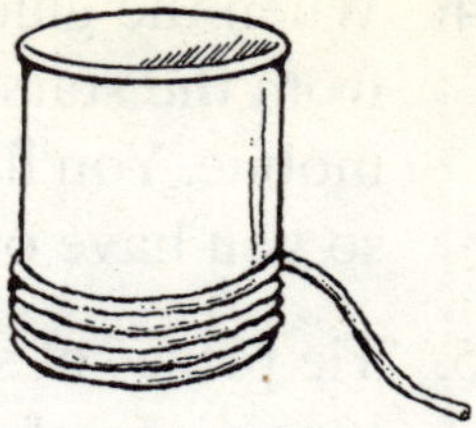

3. To make your caddy a happy caddy, glue on the two buttons for eyes. Cut a 2-inch piece of black yarn. Use the paintbrush to apply a thin line of glue on the yarn-covered can. Make a big smile! Press the black piece of yarn into the glue. Cut off any extra black yarn.

BUBBLY BATH BOTTLES

craft time: approximately 20 to 30 minutes
drying time: approximately 1 hour

In bath boutiques, a fancy bottle of bubble bath can cost a fortune. You and your friends can make up your own bottles for a few dollars.

What each girl needs:

- clear bottle (look for cool, unusual shapes, like the ones salad dressing comes in—washed out, of course)
- 2-by-3-inch adhesive name tags
- permanent waterproof color markers

- cork to fit the bottle (check kitchen supply stores)
- one large bottle of cheap bubble bath (enough to fill all the bubble-bath bottles) • funnel • 1 foot of ribbon
- variety of dried or silk flowers • strings of tiny pearls and lace ribbon • white glue

1. To decorate the bottles, first hand out a name tag to each girl. Everyone should write the name of her fancy bubble bath and decorate the label as she wishes.

2. Stick the label on the bottle. Continue to decorate it by gluing on a few dried or silk flowers or bits of lace and pearls. Finish off by tying the ribbon around the top of the bottle in a big bow.

3. Place the funnel in the bottle opening. Pour in the bubble bath up to about 1 or 2 inches from the top of the bottle. Remove the funnel and plug with the cork.

BUTTONED UP JEANS

craft time: approximately 1 hour
drying time: overnight

Send your friends off in the morning wearing their own radical, one-of-a-kind jeans.

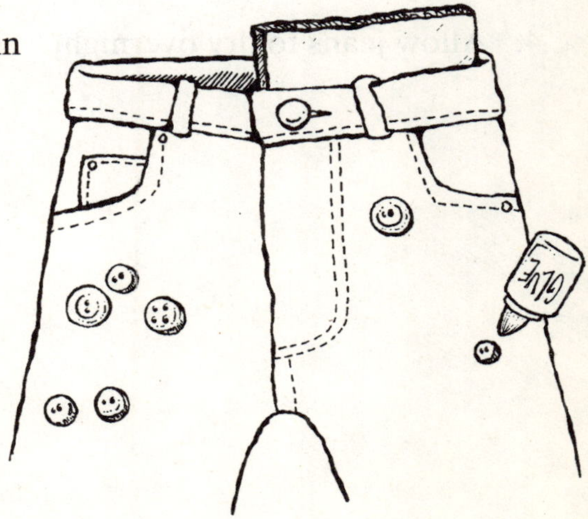

What each girl needs:

- pair of jeans (have each girl bring her own old pair) • at least 20–30 buttons

• fabric glue • piece of cardboard (cut to fit the inside of a jeans leg) • pencil • fabric paint, lace, fabric trimmings

SMART SLEEP-OVER TIP

If you're making crafts, remember to put a sheet of plastic or an old bed-sheet down on the table to catch any spills.

1. Make sure the jeans are clean. Insert the cardboard between the jeans material so the glue doesn't seep through and glue your jeans together.
2. With the fabric glue, affix buttons in a random pattern—except on the back pockets, where it would make it very uncomfortable to sit!
3. Trace a design of your initials on a leg of the jeans with a pencil. Glue the buttons along the traced lines. Use fabric paint to outline your button design, or add lace and other fabric trimmings around and behind your buttons.
4. Allow jeans to dry overnight.

Chapter 7

MAKING IT TILL MIDNIGHT . . . AND BEYOND

The best part of a sleep-over is when we stay up late and talk.

Nita P., age 9, San Antonio, Texas

Everyone knows the best part of a sleep-over party is staying up late. So what do you do to keep your eyes open, as well as everyone else's? More activities! After midnight some heads may start to nod. That's okay. But for those girls who are just getting going at midnight, here are some ideas that won't wake the whole house!

Sleeping Beauties

Give each other the beauty treatment and have fun, too. Use these ideas to baby yourself from head to toe and wake up pretty as a picture.

HAIR

Want to have a different look in the morning? Try these tricks.

Curls—Cut some fabric into 1-by-6-inch pieces. Dampen hair by running a wet brush through it. Hold a piece of fabric close to your head and wrap a strand of hair around it. Then tie it—an extra pair of hands is a big help when you tie. Next morning you'll have a head of curls.

Waves—Dampen hair. Part down the middle. Braid 2-inch sections of hair and secure each with an elastic band. Be sure to start the braids as close to your scalp as you can. The more braids you make, the more waves you'll have. By morning you'll be ready to show off your new 'do.

HANDS

For the softest hands on the block, try this sure remedy. Massage petroleum jelly all over your hands. Slip on a pair of cotton gloves. Wear them for at least an hour (or while you watch a video).

FEET

Don't forget your feet. They deserve pampering too. Slather on your favorite hand lotion all over your feet. Slip on a pair of clean cotton socks. Wear to bed. By morning your feet will be as soft as your hands.

PJ Fashion Show

Tell each girl ahead of time to bring an assortment of nightgowns or pajamas to model. Encourage them to mix and match outfits. Or have them add interesting touches, such as a nightgown with its own bedbugs (plastic creepy-crawlies attached to the nightgown). Give out awards for the goofiest, coolest, and most colorful PJs.

The Trading Boutique

Here's a chance to add clothes and accessories to your closet without spending any money. Go through your room and pick out things you don't wear anymore. Is there a pair of sunglasses you're tired of? A blouse that no longer fits? Ask your friends to weed out their closets and dressers too, and to bring those items they don't want anymore for a midnight trading boutique. Make sure you all get okays from your moms. It's better than a two-for-one sale at your favorite store!

Finish the Horror Story

Stories of werewolves, ghosts, and madmen are sure to keep you up all night. In this activity, everyone has a chance to add to the story. To start, have everyone sit in a circle. Pick one person to be the leader. She gets the flashlight and can sit anyplace within the circle, even in the center. The leader drapes a sheet around her shoulders. Turn off the light so the only illumination is from the flashlight shining up on the leader's face.

The leader begins the horror story. It should be something that sparks everyone's imagination. At the point when the story gets interesting, the leader stops. She points the flashlight onto one of the other guests. Make sure everyone has a chance to add to the story.

The following three story starters will get you rolling . . . if you dare.

The Wrong Stop—One day I had to take the bus home. I thought it was my normal bus, but it wasn't. After I realized my mistake, I got off at the next stop. It was right in front of an old graveyard. I thought I could take a shortcut by cutting across the graveyard. This was a bad mistake. It was like a maze in there. Then suddenly, right in front of me, from an unmarked grave, came . . .

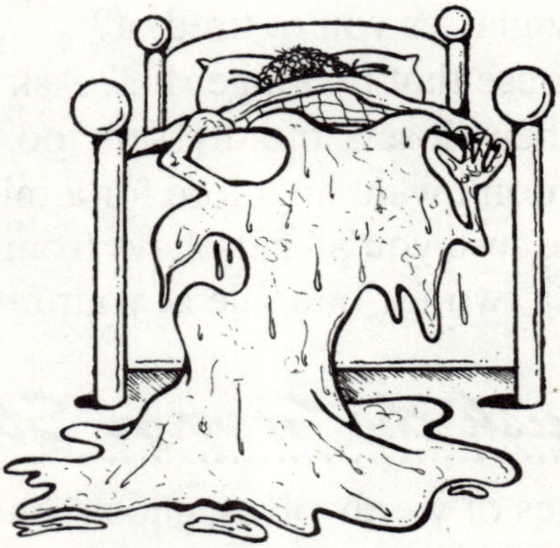

Camp Revenge—There was this girl at summer camp who really liked to scare the campers. Her favorite story to tell was about the monster who lived at the bottom of the lake. She would put slimy algae on some of the campers' beds, then she'd tell them they were marked as the monster's next victims. One night she decided to take a swim by herself. She hadn't noticed the algae laying at the foot of her bed. When she dived into the water . . .

The Dummy—When I was younger I used to like watching this ventriloquist on TV. His name was Arty, and his dummy was named Mr. Brilliant. The dummy always had the smart lines, and Arty said the stupid ones. One day Arty and Mr. Brilliant were scheduled to appear at the local mall. I got my mom to take me down there. After the show, I had to have Arty's autograph. I sneaked back to the dressing room, and immediately I knew something was wrong. Then I heard . . .

SHARE THE FRIGHT

If a high dose of fear is what you crave, have your friends bring their favorite scary-story books. Take turns reading the most frightening parts.

Romancing the Story

Do you love to read a good romance novel? Have you ever thought of writing one? It's not hard with this game.

1. First, name fifteen categories and after each, have every girl write down a word from the category to include in her romance story. Here are some category ideas: the name of a city, a color, a type of music or song, a TV show, a class at school, a favorite food, a movie, a candy bar, and an activity to do after school.
2. Then have them write down a name for the hero and the heroine.
3. Have everyone pass her romance list to the girl on her left. Give everyone ten minutes to use the words and names to write a story.
4. Take turns reading the stories aloud. Decide who has the most romantic tale. Now create a love story together. But be sure to take notes—you just might have the next bestseller!

Dream On

At some point the fun and games will stop and everyone at your sleep-over will be ready to actually sleep. And sleep means dreams. Before you drop off into dreamland, why not share some of your past dreams with your friends and discover what they mean. Dream analysts say our dreams tell us something about ourselves. Your local library probably carries a dream dictionary. Look under the subject of dreams. In the meantime, check out these symbols and see what you're dreaming about:

Animals—Dreaming about animals could mean that you need to get out and free the wild side of you.

Baby—If you dream about a baby, it means you're going through some new situations. It can also mean you feel as helpless as a baby about something in your life.

Clown—When you dream about clowns, it means you see yourself as a fun-loving person. A deeper meaning might be that you're trying to cover up something that's making you unhappy.

Falling—If you've ever had a dream about falling, it probably means you feel something in your life is out of control.

Flying—If you dream about flying or even flying in an airplane, it means you're happy. It also might mean you've recently solved a problem on your own.

Missing a bus (or plane, train, etc.)—Any dream where you're late for an appointment or bus could mean you're anxious to get moving. Maybe you can't wait to start rehearsal for the school play.

Taking a test—It can mean that you are avoiding doing something you need to do, and you know it is going to catch up with you.

Toys—Good luck is coming your way—unless your dream is about broken toys. In that case, you may have a tendency to act like a baby sometimes.

SMART SLEEP-OVER TIP

Have a bunch of board games or a few puzzles available to play when you've finished your other planned activities.

My favorite game after midnight is a murder mystery game on my computer's CD-ROM. Everyone gathers around and tries to figure out the clues.

Abby B., age 12, Topeka, Kansas

Best Video Rentals

Late at night is the best time to watch a video. The ones listed below are all fun. Which one you watch depends upon whether you want to scream, laugh, or sigh. Always make sure the video you want is rated PA—Parent Approved!

SCARE YOUR SOCKS OFF (ALMOST)

Beetlejuice (1988, PG, 92 minutes). A renegade spirit named Beetlejuice (Michael Keaton) helps an ultra-nice ghost couple rid their home of a new, obnoxious family.

Gremlins (1984, PG, 106 minutes). A teenager (Zack Galligan) gets a new pet and a warning: Don't expose him to bright light, don't ever get him wet, and don't ever, ever feed him after midnight!

Poltergeist (1982, PG, 114 minutes). A young family face terror as a poltergeist abducts their five-year-old (Heather O'Rourke) through the TV screen.

TICKLE YOUR FUNNY BONE

Big (1988, PG, 102 minutes). A twelve-year-old boy wishes he were "big." Then he wakes up the next day and finds he's a thirty-year-old man (Tom Hanks)!

Who Framed Roger Rabbit (1988, PG, 103 minutes). Animated and live-action characters share the spotlight in this mystery about a private eye (Bob Hoskins) trying to clear goofy cartoon character Roger Rabbit of a crime.

Tootsie (1982, PG, 116 minutes). Dustin Hoffman plays a struggling actor who disguises himself as a woman just to get an acting part on a soap opera.

MIDNIGHT SNACKS

When the midnight munchies strike, try one of these great snacks.

Mini-pizzas–Spread canned pizza sauce on a split, toasted English muffin. Top with cheese. Put in the microwave for 30 seconds.

Popcorn–Top with melted butter (or use butter-flavored nonstick cooking spray). Sprinkle with dried pizza seasoning and parmesan cheese. Mix in a big bowl to coat.

Banana Cookies–Slice a banana into thick coins. Put each piece between two vanilla wafers.

Fruity Shake–For each fruity shake you'll need ½ cup sliced soft fruit (strawberries, bananas, or peaches), ⅓ cup of apple juice, ¾ cup of milk, and four or five ice cubes. Place all ingredients into a blender and whip until thick and smooth.

AH, HOW ROMANTIC!

Beauty and the Beast (1991, G, 85 minutes). Disney's animated version of a classic fairy tale. Beauty sees beyond the outer appearance of the Beast and falls in love with him.

Roxanne (1987, PG, 107 minutes). Small town fire chief (Steve Martin) thinks he's too ugly for the beautiful Roxanne (Daryl Hannah), but he helps another young man romance her.

Romeo and Juliet (1968, PG, 138 minutes). The Shakespeare classic about two young lovers who are kept apart by their families.

> *After we've played all our games, we give each other manicures.*
>
> Katie V., age 11, Trenton, New Jersey

SMART SLEEP-OVER TIP

Well-traveled hallways and other areas should be lit all night for guests. Use night-lights or low wattage bulbs (25 watts) in lamps. Have a flashlight handy just in case the lights burn out or someone wants to make a raid on the refrigerator.

Chapter 8
GOOD MORNING, SLEEPYHEAD!

The morning after my sleep-over I like to plan a special breakfast.

Stephanie G., age 11, Huntsville, Alabama

The fun doesn't have to stop once you wake up. Just put the same thought into the morning after as you did into the night before. But at a slower pace, please. Not everyone wakes up bright-eyed and bushy-tailed!

Breakfast of Champions

Starting your day off with a healthy breakfast is as good advice the morning after a sleep-over as it is on regular days. But the meal doesn't have to be boring. Here are some ideas for a nutritious breakfast that are still fun.

THE DRY CEREAL TASTE TEST

Pick four or five cereals beforehand for this taste test. In the morning, invite your friends to sit around the table. Pour each cereal into a paper cup for every guest, labeled by letter. Hand out the letter A cereals. Have each girl eat it and write down her rating of 1 through 5. Also have each girl write down what kind of ceral she thinks it is. Do this with every cereal. The girl who can correctly guess the most cereals wins.

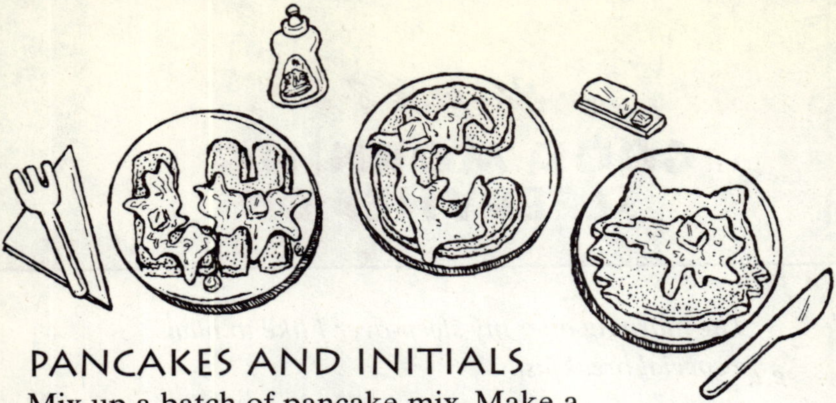

PANCAKES AND INITIALS

Mix up a batch of pancake mix. Make a thin batter by mixing equal parts of pancake mix and water (or follow your mix's recipe for crepes). Put the mix into a plastic squeeze bottle, like a washed mustard bottle. You'll need an extra-large hole to squirt out the pancake batter (get your mom to cut a larger hole in the tip). Let each of your guests squirt out some of the pancake mix in the shape of their initials or any other shapes they would like. Cook as you would normal pancakes.

GET UP AND MOVE

Get your day off to a healthy start. Put on your favorite exercise and fitness tapes and get your friends up on their feet. Or try something a little different, like a yoga tape. It's always more fun to exercise with a friend. When you're finished, sit down to a healthy breakfast. Try bran muffins and orange juice, or your favorite granola covered with fresh berries and skim milk.

We stay up so late, nobody ever gets up before 11 A.M.!

Hildy M., age 12, New York, New York

Saying Thanks

As the sleep-over winds down, thank your parents for allowing you to have such a great party. You'll be surprised at how much even a small thank-you gesture will mean to them. There are lots of ways to do this:

Give a thank-you card—Store-bought is nice, but why not make one yourself? It can be one of your morning-after activities. All you need is a large piece of poster board, markers, and imagination. Fold the poster board in half, bringing together the two short ends. Draw a few designs and make sure all your guests sign the card.

Say it with a song—It may seem silly, but why not serenade your parents? Besides, it'll give you a chance to show them it was more than mindless noise you were making the night before.

Make* them *breakfast in bed—This may take a little organization on your part, but with your buddies helping, you'll make a big impression.

Just say it—It doesn't cost anything, and when said sincerely, it means a lot.

A Clean Sweep

Your friends are all gone, so what's left for you to do? Just take a look around the house. It's a bad idea to leave the house a mess for your parents to clean. As hostess, it's your responsibility to tidy up. Here are some simple clean-up tips to make the task go faster:

- ✔ Don't put it off. The longer you wait to get started cleaning, the harder it'll be to get up and get it done.
- ✔ Put on some music. Your favorite tunes will make the time pass more quickly.
- ✔ Clean the rooms used by other family members first. They'll appreciate it.
- ✔ Don't get distracted. Finish one job and move on to the next. It'll be done before you know it.

It's Over

Your friends are gone. You've cleaned up. You're so tired you're ready to drop in your tracks. But before you crawl into your bed to rest up, take a few minutes to think about what kind of time you had. What was the best part? What didn't work? How can it be better next time? Now you'll have experience to draw from to help all your future ultimate sleep-overs!